# GUILDFORD & VILLAGES
## THEN AND NOW

# GUILDFORD & VILLAGES
## THEN AND NOW

DAVID ROSE

breedon **books**
**PUBLISHING**

First published in Great Britain in 2003 by

The Breedon Books Publishing Company Limited

Breedon House, 3 The Parker Centre,

Derby, DE21 4SZ.

ISBN 1 85983 382 9

Printed and bound by Butler & Tanner,

Frome, Somerset, England.

Cover printing by Lawrence-Allen Colour Printers,

Weston-super-Mare, Somerset, England.

# Contents

# INTRODUCTION

I have been fascinated by my home town of Guildford for as long as I can remember – and curious to see what the town and the surrounding villages looked like in years gone by.

Fortunately, the picture postcard photographers of the first half of the 20th century have left a wonderful record. It's believed that just about every town-centre street, village and byway in the UK was photographed and published as a picture postcard sometime during that period.

As you will see within this book, professional photographers as well as amateurs have done an excellent job recording streets and buildings – just before they were pulled down or if they made an interesting or enchanting view.

We see change all around us and learn to accept it – particularly in our town centres. We may like to think that the picturesque villages that surround them have managed to escape unwanted change.

This book sets out to discover what really has and has not altered, comparing views from the early days of photography in the 19th century through to the end of the 20th century, and how they look today. It may shock you to see places that you thought hadn't changed for years and, on the other hand, leave you wondering how some places have escaped the ravages of modern development!

This book is also the result of two questions I am often asked as I regularly speak to people about local history matters. When are you going to produce a book that includes images of the villages surrounding Guildford? And what about one that shows past and present views? It seemed a good idea to combine both and the result is Guildford & Villages Then and Now.

The book begins with a look at the town centre followed by its outskirts. I have then chosen views from around today's borough of Guildford including the RHS Garden at Wisley. Furthermore, I have also included pictures from one or two places that are technically just outside the borough, but are closely associated with Guildford.

As always, it has only been possible to work with the material available at the time. It goes without saying that the villages deemed the most picturesque have had the most pictures taken of them over the years and therefore have survived in the greatest numbers.

The majority of the older photographs are from my own collection, however I would like to thank the following who kindly loaned pictures from their collections: John Young, for pictures of Bramley, Wonersh, Eashing, Compton, and several of Shalford; the *Surrey Advertiser*; Sue Thompson and John Battye of the Royal Horticultural Society at Wisley; Bernard Parke; Peter Phillips; Liz Thurhurst; G. Rogers; Carol Brown; The Guildford Institute of the University of Surrey; Bill Nixon; Geoffrey Crates, George and Christine Smith; and The Guildford Society.

I would also like to thank John Sutton for information about the Onslow Street area of Guildford, postcard dealers and collectors Tim Notley and Tim Winter who have tracked down many interesting cards for me, Ron Hill for some useful guidance about the history of Wonersh and the Pepperpot, Albert Carter for identifying a view in Albury, Brenda Smith for a view in Shatford, and to the numerous members of local history societies in the area from whom I have gleaned much knowledge.

With the odd exception, all the modern-day photographs were taken by myself between March and June 2003. They were taken with a Canon PowerShot A20 digital camera. This excellent piece of equipment displays an instant image of the view just taken and helped no end in lining up the then and the now "shots".

The intention was to take a view at as near as possible the exact same spot as the earlier photographer did. Therefore, I was not concerned with taking a picturesque-style photograph. For me, it did not matter whether the view was filled with lines of parked cars. If however, a view of a specific and perhaps important building was obscured by trees, on one or two occasions I moved a few paces to the left or right.

Although the picture postcards of yesteryear may be full of nostalgia, it must be remembered that when they were taken the photographer of the day would often include bystanders and vehicles within his pictures. I have done just the same. I make no excuses in admitting that my daughter Bryony appears in several of the photographs; and you will even spot my silver Rover 200 in some of the views as well as my bicycle. Cycling was the easiest method of transport around the town centre!

One thing does seem to be different to when the photographers of yesteryear were at work. When they came down the street with their large glass-plate camera, tripod and box of accessories, this novel event often resulted in a crowd gathering to watch. Nowadays, we are so used to people taking pictures or filming with camcorders, that hardly anyone bothered to stop to ask what I was doing as I went on my rounds.

David Rose
Summer 2003

# AROUND THE TOWN CENTRE

Swept away: The old town bridge was all but destroyed by timber brought down stream from Moon's yard in the floods of February 1900. A pipeline appears to be the only item linking both banks of the river.

A new bridge was opened in 1902, but was replaced in 1985 by the one that spans the River Wey today.

The dawn of the motor age. However, horse-drawn traffic outnumbers motor vehicles by at least six to one in this view that looks up the High Street from the town bridge.

The buildings nearest to the bridge have long since gone, today it serves as a footbridge only.

Come on in the water's lovely! More floods at the bottom of the High Street, this time in January 1928.

As many local people know only too well, this part of the town has seen the River Wey burst its banks on numerous occasions – not least in the last few years. A plaque on the wall of St Nicolas Church (right) marks the height of the September 1968 flood waters.

There have been a number of occupants of the small strip of land beside the town bridge near St Nicolas Church. It was once occupied by stonemasons Arthur Moon & Sons, followed by Cuthbert's Garage. There was even a plan submitted to build a theatre here! The White House building was constructed in the 1950s and, according to the 1967 *Kelly's Directory*, was then occupied by Wells & Phillpot solicitors. This view dates from March 1984 when the building was empty and boarded up.

It became The White House pub at the end of 1994 and is a popular establishment run by the Chiswick brewers Fuller, Smith & Turner.

This was the view from the town bridge looking towards Millmead in November 1933. John Moon & Son's timber yard was on east bank of the river (left) while on the opposite bank stonemasons Arthur Moon & Sons, had its yard.

Debenhams' store has occupied the timber yard site for nearly 40 years and an area of open space planted with willow trees graces the opposite bank of the river.

A picture from the days when you could drive along Friary Street and turn left or right into the High Street. On one corner stood John Collier, men's tailors; and on the other, in the 1950s, a tobacconist known as The Cigar Stores. In the 1960s it became Lewis of Westminster.

Friary Street has long been pedestrianised and the former John Collier building has had a succession of occupants – lately a bar and cafe. In early 2003 the builders and shopfitters were in again with another makeover for a new retailer.

At one time you could park your car in the Angel Hotel yard. The famous High Street inn has a long history going back to the 16th century.

Shops and cafes now make this a vibrant spot in the town centre and it is still a cut-through for pedestrians from the High Street to North Street.

Union Jack flags hang from almost every building in the High Street to herald the silver jubilee of George V in 1935. On the left is the entrance to the Picture Playhouse arcade that contained a theatre, shops, a club and winter gardens.

Banning vehicles from the High Street during the daytime has helped make Guildford High Street one of the most popular shopping centres in the South of England. However, some criticise the dominance of the multi-national stores citing, for example, a lack of food shops. Tunsgate Square currently occupies the site of the former Picture Playhouse and arcade.

Look there's something missing! A rare view of the High Street with the Guildhall clock removed. Restoration work was carried out in 1934, making it necessary to remove the clock, and between October 23, 1940, and September 6, 1945, it was again removed for safe keeping during the Second World War. Unfortunately this photograph is not dated.

The High Street early one Sunday morning in May 2003, with the old clock resplendent in its position projecting from the Guildhall. It is the symbol of Guildford and this view is known throughout the world.

The White Hart Inn was pulled down in 1905 and Sainsbury's opened a branch in its place on Guildford High Street. This late 1920s picture shows the store's fleet of delivery vehicles. The service carried on until 1955.

Now called Sainsbury's Central, it is one food store that remains in the town centre. How many people notice the plaque between the two bay windows? It is a reminder of when the building was a coaching inn.

William Massey's pharmacy dominates the corner of Chertsey Street and the upper High Street in this 1920s view. There was also a branch at the bottom of the High Street near the town bridge. According to the writing beneath the window of Kendrick's shop, next door, it sold Crest china and postcards, both now very collectable.

The building on the corner in the previous photograph had gone by the early 1960s and its replacement still stands today. The pavement has been widened around the statue of Archbishop George Abbot.

A neat line is formed by the buildings on the left and Holy Trinity Church at the top of the High Street. A giant pair of spectacles can be seen on the white-washed frontage of Horstmann's opticians.

Sculptor Faith Winter's statue of Archbishop George Abbot, unveiled in 1993, is the the only real difference in these two views.

A view of the upper High Street looking down towards Ram Corner. By 1913 the traffic congestion was so bad here that the pub was pulled down and the road widened.

A rather pleasing bank chambers building in a neo-Georgian style was built on the site in the 1920s. Seen here, the right-hand side of the upper High Street had been redeveloped by the 1960s, but the other side has not changed a great deal. Another early morning photograph.

Dating from the 16th century, the Royal Grammar School is a well known Guildford landmark building. This night-time shot was taken during the silver jubilee of George V in 1935. The town was lit up with additional electric lighting to celebrate the occasion.

The Royal Grammar School may not be lit at night nowadays, but its facade is whitewashed making it stand out rather well.

Changes are seen taking place in London Road with the junction of Epsom Road and the upper High Street in April 1934. It would not be long before the Prudential Buildings were built along Epsom Road and Crow Bros motor garage ceased to operate from here.

Changes are taking place again in 2003. The Prudential Buildings have recently gone and will soon be replaced by luxury apartments.

Feature films were not the only kind of entertainment at the Odeon cinema in Epsom Road. During the 1960s it was a popular concert venue and was packed out when, in 1963, the Beatles played two shows in one day. Among other pop bands who played there in those days were the Rolling Stones.

The former cinema building with an art deco-style frontage, had largely been cleared away by the spring of 2003, along with the Prudential Buildings.

Dene Road, off London Road, is a good example of late Victorian housing. Many of the large houses in this part of Guildford would have had one or two live-in servants. Today, a large percentage of these homes have been divided up into flats.

The Dene Road houses now face the Guildford Civic, but for how much longer? Plans for its redevelopment here or on a new site are still undecided after much wrangling in recent years. The line of trees are a marked difference.

In 1983 work began on an extension at the rear of Abbot's Hospital to create further accommodation at the home for elderly people.

Architects Nye Saunders & Partners designed the 12 flats, seen here from North Street, that blend harmoniously with the original building that dates from 1619.

The Crown is another of Guildford's lost pubs – demolished for road widening. There can be few alive today who can recall this Friary Brewery watering hole. To the left can be seen the premises of Pimms – the removal firm and undertakers.

Another of Guildford's less eye-catching developments occupies the former Pimms site. The shop on the extreme left was once the Horse & Groom pub, where five people lost their lives when it was bombed by the IRA in 1974.

The Cloth Hall was built in the 17th century as a manufactory in an attempt to revive Guildford's once prosperous woollen industry. The building later became Abbot's School and is now associated with garments once more. They are sold there under the name of the Edinburgh Woollen Mill.

An extremely plain building has replaced the one previously at right angles to the Cloth Hall. The pedestrian walkway Jeffries Passage, with its own shops, is named after Henry Jeffries who had a pharmacy at the High Street end.

The engine house of the town's fire brigade in North Street soon after it was built in 1872. The brigade moved to the present fire station in Ladymead, in 1937.

The old fire station building has seen some alterations over the years – note the second storey added over the section in Ward Street. It is now a public lavatory that had a thorough refit and makeover in 2002.

This view not only shows the fire station building but the Royal Arms Temperance Hotel, built by the rector of Stoke-next-Guildford, the Rev Francis Paynter, and opened in 1881 to provide non-alcoholic refreshments.

The hotel was not the success that the good rector had hoped for. Today the ground floor on the corner is occupied by the Royal Bank of Scotland. The upper floors are the home of the Guildford Institute of the University of Surrey. The organisation can be traced back to 1834 when a group of Guildford citizens formed a mechanics' institute "for the promotion of useful knowledge among the working classes". Although it deviated from its original aims somewhat, the institute grew and moved into the former hotel in 1891 and extended the building along Ward Street. Now linked with the University of Surrey, the institute houses a very interesting lending library. It also has a fascinating collection of old photographs, scrap books and other historical material relating to Guildford. Lectures, courses, conferences and exhibitions are held there, plus there is a vegetarian restaurant open on weekday lunchtimes.

Greenhouses of a market garden firm once stood here in Martyr Road.

In 1937, the *Surrey Advertiser* moved from Market Street to brand new print works and offices in Martyr Road. The newspaper moved to Stoke Mill in 1999. The empty building is seen here in February 2001.

The newspaper's art-deco style headquarters and the later extension that eventually housed the press were demolished in 2002. New offices, in the style of the former Advertiser House building, should rise from the brick rubble.

March 1983 and a building at the junction of North Street and Leapale Road that became known as Co-op Corner. Previously this building had been the Borough Halls, and then a theatre as well as a Co-op store. The coloured panel featured a man and a woman, two children, scenes from the town including Guildford Cathedral, and a clock.

A fairly plain red-brick building stands on the site today. It is nowhere near as pleasing as the Bargate stone building of earlier times.

Swan Lane not long before the Seven Stars pub was wrecked by an IRA bomb that exploded on Saturday, October 5, 1974. Further along can be seen the Guildford Dolls' Hospital toy shop. The author can well remember this store and also a huge pair of denim jeans that hung above the entrance to a menswear shop (just visible) on the opposite side of the lane.

The pub eventually became an off-licence but is currently occupied by a coffee shop and a tea importers. On the left-hand side, Boots has extended into many of the properties here and linked them through to its High Street store.

Guildford Fire Brigade pose at the end of Woodbridge Road, with North Street away on the right, in a photograph from the late 1860s.

Today's photograph has been angled slightly to the right of the previous one to show the recent large glass structure that is a House of Fraser store. It is seen rising above the North Street shops.

The spire of the Methodist church dwarfs the other buildings here in North Street in about 1910. The church was pulled down in 1973, and today Guildford's Methodists worship in a church in Woodbridge Road.

The lamp-posts may be styled on those of an earlier era but the security cameras on the building on the right-hand side are modern and an increasingly necessary addition to the town centre. Something our forebears could not have dreamed of.

What goes up sometimes soon comes down! And this was the story of the Blackfriars, a short-lived pub at the entrance to the Friary shopping centre. The outside drinking area (it could never have been described as a pub garden) is seen here, under construction, in 1981.

Within seven years it had gone following alterations to the centre to create more shops. Changes have taken place on the opposite side of the road too, with the White Lion Walk development.

A weigh bridge and attendant's kiosk once stood at the bottom of North Street. The Dennis motor works can be seen on the left in the background. It became the Rodboro Buildings in 1919 when its new occupants, the Rodboro Boot & Shoe Company, moved in.

The Friary Centre (and more security cameras) dominate today's view along with a busy taxi rank.

After the First World War and as a thank you for its war savings efforts Guildford was presented with a tank! It was brought by rail to London Road station, but once unloaded it broke down. The mayor and dignitaries were left stranded, as it should have rumbled through the town and arrived at its new home at the bottom of North Street where they were waiting. Eventually, they dashed up to the station for the handing-over ceremony. The tank was mobilised a few days later and finally reached its destination. It remained there until 1923 when it was cut up for scrap.

It is difficult to find the exact spot from which the accompanying photograph was taken. However, this is roughly the same view that now looks towards Phoenix Court and the entrance for shop delivery vehicles.

The Quadrant buildings in Onslow Street with the Plaza bingo hall just out of view to the right. During the 1980s the Olympic Cafe – serving both English and Greek food – was here as well as The Old Curiosity Shoppe. Unlike some towns, Guildford never appears to have been a centre for shops selling antiques and collectables.

Local businessman Michel Harper now has bars and his nightclub The Drink on this corner. The borough council has recently designated Onslow Street a "conservation area" in the hope of protecting it from further changes of usage and drastic alterations.

The Onslow Street bus station pictured in 1975. Alder Valley was the company that was formed from the amalgamation of the Aldershot & District Traction Co., and Thames Valley Buses – itself a subsidiary of the National Bus Company.

This is now quite a large area of open space – unusual in the centre of Guildford where land is always at a premium. The former Electricity Works is now the town's Electric Theatre and the upper floor of the Rodboro Buildings is the home of the Academy of Contemporary Music. The young people seen congregating here are students waiting for their afternoon classes to begin.

Plenty of greenery beside the River Wey seen here in a photograph dating from July 1983. At this time Bridge Street was closed while repairs were being made to the bridge itself. The land to the left, at the back of the buildings on Farnham Road, had not yet been cleared for redevelopment.

Offices of the company Standard Life Healthcare are now beside the river on the left of this picture. The river frontage has been improved no end, but many feel it will always be cut off from the town as long as the gyratory system is in place.

This view of Sutton Buildings, in Onslow Street near the junction with Woodbridge Road, and the majority of the accompanying older photographs, were taken by Peter Phillips not long before the redevelopment of this area in the early 1970s. Seen here, from left, is Cooke's travel agents. Next, for many years a tobacconist and a sweet shop. The last trader was a Mr French. Directly above these two shops were offices known as Market Chambers. The next shop along was once the premises of Chas Sutton & Co, selling ladies and gents clothing, footwear and drapery. In 1950 the business closed and Hills, a furnishing company, became the tenants.

A view that is entirely different today!

Tribe & Robinson's Onslow Building Works' premises at the junction of Laundry Road and Onslow Street. The electric firm Bowden & Higlett was also part of the "Tribe" empire.

Today beyond the trees is the magistrates' court and behind that Guildford police station.

A view of some rather ramshackle buildings in Laundry Road. The sign for Albert Ward & Sons' blacksmith can be seen and the cars are parked in what was once the cattle market.

Laundry Road was re-aligned when the redevelopment took place, but this is basically the same view.

A glimpse of Onslow Street looking towards Woodbridge Road and St Saviour's Church. On the right is the City Cafe and French the tobacconist. The building directly behind the Land-Rover was St Saviour's Church Hall.

The church is the key building in finding this location. This view was taken standing on the long concrete mound covered with cobblestone that now runs between the pavement and the road.

Onslow Street, and the area around, was once a community all of its own. The 1959 edition of *Kelly's Directory of Guildford & Godalming* lists, among other traders on the east side, butcher Philip Turner, tool driller J. Parsons, the Friary Recreation Club, the St Mary's Lodge of the Oddfellows, and the trade entrance and showrooms of Angel, Son & Gray Ltd.

The delivery vehicle entrance to the Friary centre is beneath the Alders store sign. The Drink nightclub can be seen in the distance. This was the Plaza in the accompanying picture, and is the key to aligning the two views.

This part of Onslow Street became rather run down in the final years before redevelopment. By May 1976, when this photograph was taken, the old Friary Meux brewery site behind these buildings had been cleared as had the former Angel, Son & Grey site further along the road.

The side of the Friary centre and the walkway to the Bedford Road car park now dominates the view.

The Salvation Army's citadel in Laundry Road was a rather unique looking structure with the organisation's crest making an attractive addition to the front of the building.

You would never know what had previously stood here and now a second office block is going up on the site.

A fairly quiet Woodbridge Road with Leas Road joining it on the right. These buildings were known as Wellington Place and the property on the corner was once the home of the Guildford branch of St John Ambulance.

The building that is the Guildford branch of the Salvation Army is now on the corner of Leas Road, with Guildford police station, in Mary Road, towering behind.

College Road joins Woodbridge Road on the left of this photograph and the premises here was occupied by Godfrey Holmes, motor factors. It had previously been The Furniture Mart. Next door were the offices of Britannic Assurance and then the auctioneers and estate agents Weller Eggar, followed by the West Surrey Farmers' Association.

Once again, apart from St Saviour's Church, everything from the previous photograph has been swept away.

The Prince of Wales pub, that was for many years run by the Boyce family. They were also well known for their catering business. The pub was pulled down in 1972.

The office building that replaced the pub still stands although the shop on the ground floor was for some years the showrooms of Romans, a motor dealer.

Guildford railway station seen from the Farnham Road bridge in the early 1900s. This was very much how the station looked for 100 years.

Some of the platforms have been lengthened and the new station buildings date to 1988.

Looking across to what was platform 1 in about 1910, now, of course, platform 2. Beneath the canopy there are a plethora of signs and advertisements just visible on the walls of the waiting rooms and refreshment room.

Gone are the old-style station benches replaced by modern seats and electronic display screens keep customers (no longer passengers) up to date with train times.

Guildford railway station in 1976 and the once ubiquitous cars of the age! At this time the main entrance for passengers was further along to the right.

The new Guildford railway station won a design award. Unfortunately at about the point where the previous picture was taken, the new buildings do not make a pretty picture!

Crowds line the pavement from the entrance of the railway station and along Bridge Street hoping to catch a glimpse of the Queen as she passes in her car. She was on her way to visit the Women's Royal Army Corps camp at Stoughton in 1964.

The redevelopment of the railway station and its approach in the late 1980s have not made it easy to find the exact spot where the original photographer stood. Many buildings in the vicinity have gone, including the Napoleon Hotel, in Farnham Road.

These whitewashed cottages with steps to their doors do not seem characteristic of Guildford at all. However, they once stood in Park Street.

Rather bland offices replaced the cottages, although a few doors down one or two older buildings remain, one currently occupied by an Indian restaurant.

A night-time view of Quarry Street in the mid 1950s. The building on the left once housed the Guildford Dispensary, opened in 1860, offering a medical and surgical service to outpatients. It was the forerunner of the Royal Surrey County Hospital.

The Kings Head pub looks much the same, but internally is much altered. In the 1970s it was a very popular haunt of young people who followed the local music scene. Musician Tony Backhurst and his band, House, regularly played at the pub. The signpost on the corner is a recent addition and the building on the left is current Olivo's Italian restaurant.

Quarry Street about 100 years ago. Note the mature trees in St Mary's churchyard.

The facades of the buildings have hardly altered and now there is a pleasant view of the town's oldest church.

Castle Arch has been a popular choice for picture postcard photographers over the last 100 years. This one was taken sometime between the two world wars.

The 13th-century arch is a treasured part of Guildford's history. The building on the right has been the home of the Surrey Archaeological Society since 1898.

The Castle Keep must come a close second to the Guildhall clock as the symbol of Guildford. It stands in grounds that were landscaped and opened to the public in 1888 to mark the 50th anniversary of the coronation of Queen Victoria.

Periodic restoration work ensures that the keep is preserved as an ancient monument. However, when it was built in the 12th century it would probably have had whitewashed walls so that it could be seen for miles around. Today, only those playing bowls are allowed on the green in the foreground.

A sunny day in 1935 looking down Quarry Street towards Shalford Road and the Jolly Farmer pub. This is one of many photographs of the town taken on a Box Brownie camera during the mid 1930s by pupils of the Central School. It was a project that has left us with a remarkable collection of pictures from that era.

A different group of buildings stand on the left-hand side today and Quarry Street has long been a one-way street for motor vehicles.

If ever there was to be the perfect picture postcard view of the River Wey in Guildford, it would have to be one featuring the Jolly Farmer. This shows the original pub before it was replaced in 1913 by the present building.

Today the big breweries and pub owning companies are forever re-branding their products and services. This often involves the changing of pub names. So the Jolly Farmer is now the Weyside. Apt maybe, but rather bland?

Upstream from Leroy's boathouse there was at one time a wooden footbridge. It was replaced in 1934 when its timbers rotted.

Today's bridge gracefully spans the river and is the point of access for many people taking a stroll along the riverbank.

The Central School's project of its pupils taking photographs around the town would not have been complete without a photograph of the school itself. It is seen here in about 1935.

Today the buildings comprise of an adult education centre and Guildford's Harvey Gallery.

# THE OUTSKIRTS OF GUILDFORD

Before Farnham Road was constructed, travellers in and out of Guildford would have used the road up over The Mount. The photographer of this 1920s picture has made it up the steep incline and the view looks back over the town.

The road is now made up to this point and houses have been added on the left. The Mount cemetery is away to the right.

From the outskirts looking in, and cabbages and churches appear to dominate this late 19th century view of the town a short distance from Mount Street. St Nicolas Church is in the middle foreground, with St Mary's away to the right. On the skyline can be seen the tower of Holy Trinity.

It was possible to obtain this photograph by pointing the camera through a gap in a grille on the side of the walk-way that leads from Wodeland Avenue to the Farnham Road multi-storey car park. The previous picture, however, was probably taken several yards further back on the edge of the road itself. Nevertheless, some interesting comparisons can be made looking across the town.

An unfinished Guildford Cathedral surrounded by scaffolding in a post-Second World War view from The Mount. Work began on the red-brick structure in 1936, but the war halted the building programme. Work slowly resumed after the war but it took a lot of effort to raise funds. This was helped by local Labour politician Leslie Codd's enthusiasm to see the building completed and the sterling fund-raising by Eleanor Iredale, that included the buy-a-brick campaign.

It was consecrated in 1961, and Sir Edward Maufe's design, standing proudly on Stag Hill, can be seen for miles around and is the focal point for the Diocese of Guildford.

A Dennis Bros road-cleaning vehicle is being tested as it enters Old Palace Road from Madrid Road. The tall chimney of the Guildford Park brickworks can be seen in the background.

The houses on the right have hardly altered, but on the left the sheltered housing of Dene Court now stands where there was once a Co-op store.

A view from the forecourt of the Co-op dairy that was once a well-known landmark in Woodbridge Meadows. A single-storey office building eventually occupied the site where the shrubbery is in this picture.

The former brick-arch bridge, seen on the right of the accompanying photo, has long since gone, replaced by a new bridge. The other bridge remains but has not carried advertising on its sides for many years. Today, a PC World computer store and a Comet electrical goods store occupy the former dairy site.

Alder Valley's Guildford bus depot in Woodbridge Road seen here in May 1985. There had been a bus garage here since 1927.

All that was swept away some time ago and a kitchen manufacturer's showroom occupies the site today.

The coal-fired power station in Woodbridge Road was a monster of a building. It generated electricity from 1928 to 1968. A possible target for enemy aircraft during the Second World War, it even had its own Home Guard platoon!

Other electricity company buildings replaced the power station, but even these have stood empty for some years. At the time of writing they were being demolished to be replaced by housing.

The Avenue in Woodbridge Road was a terrace of 18 houses near the entrance to Stocton Road. It is seen here in the early 1900s, but by the 1960s had been demolished.

Nothing remains to link these two photos. The road is one of the busiest routes into town; the building beyond the roundabout is a veterinary surgery.

Work is about to begin on clearing houses along Ladymead and the industrial buildings behind to make way for today's Europa Retail Park.

Another very busy spot seen here with traffic slowing down for the lights. The car park next to the Burger King fast-food restaurant is a mecca for motor enthusiasts – as once a month on a Sunday evening it is the meeting point for the Guildford Cruise. Customised vehicles of all shapes and sizes are driven here from miles around and crowds gather to marvel at them.

The imposing Stoke Park Mansion seen here in 1977, the year of its demolition. Dating from the late 18th century, it had been a private residence and later a school.

Many believe that it should never have been pulled down. There would appear to be no trace of the former building today and a skateboard park occupies part of the site.

Model yachts large and small grace the boating pool in Stoke Park. It was created along with the paddling pool and rockery in 1935 to coincide with the silver jubilee of George V.

The pool looks much the same today. The timbers of the wooden bridge were replaced some years ago.

The once notorious Woking Road and Stoke Road roundabout near the fire station at Ladymead. A place feared by those having to negotiate it while taking their driving tests! The year is 1979.

Traffic lights have replaced the roundabout and the Parkway hotel with its restaurant and bars can just be seen on the left-hand side.

As part of the A3 diversion, tons of earth were moved to create an embankment for the new roadway. Even the course of the River Wey had to be altered in the process. This view is near Stoke Bridges on the Woking Road.

No matter how much landscaping is done, if it isn't completely covered with concrete, nature always finds a foothold and recolonises a patch of ground, as can be seen here.

A local bobby keeps a watchful eye on the picture postcard photographer as he takes this view of the bridge over the River Wey Navigation at Stoke, in about 1905.

The present bridge was built in 1926 along with its neighbouring one, away to the right. At one time traffic could turn into Riverside from Woking Road, and on at least one occasion a motorist turned too sharply and crashed through the fence and ended up in the water.

The imposing Stoke Mill in its heyday as a corn mill, circa 1900. At one time local produce would have been milled here, but in later years barges operated by the Stevens family brought wheat from the Port of London up the Thames and along the Wey Navigation.

The last grain was milled here in 1957 and the building then became a paint factory and warehouse. It was converted to spacious offices in 1989, and since 1999 has been the headquarters of the Surrey Advertiser Group of newspapers, itself a division of the Guardian Media Group.

Brothers William and Henry Parsons were wealthy Guildford drapers and when they retired they decided to pay for a home, called a hospital, for six poor widows from the parish of Stoke. The Stoke Road hospital opened in 1796, but only William saw the vision fulfilled as his brother had died three years earlier. In this Edwardian view everyone appears to be looking at the baby in the perambulator.

The graceful building has not changed its appearance at all. It is still a residence for senior citizens and today there are 13 self-contained flats and a matron's cottage.

Guildford High School in London Road a few years after it had moved here in 1893 from its first home in Haydon Place.

The school has expanded in recent years with a number of new buildings. One tree in particular has been allowed to mature.

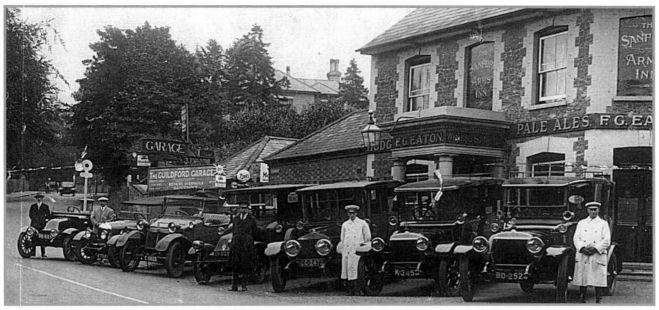

A splendid line up of motor-cars outside The Guildford Garage, next door to the Sanford Arms pub in Epsom Road. As well as offering repairs and overhauls, the sign states that the garage offered private cars for hire. BP and Pratt's motor spirit is also advertised.

Vehicles from a later era stand outside the KLG Sanford garage that replaced the earlier group of buildings.

The garage is still in business, but in 2002 the Sanford Arms became Rogues – a wine bar that had moved there after the Prudential Buildings at the town end of Epsom Road had been earmarked for demolition and redevelopment.

At one time the Guildford area was served by a number of laundries that took in and cleaned all types of garments. This is the Alexandra Laundry on the corner of Warren Road and Cooper Road. Others included Burns (also in Warren Road), the County Laundry in Weyside Road, the Guildford Laundry in Laundry Road, the Burpham Hand Laundry and the Bramley Hygienic Laundry.

About 20 years separate these two views and homes have been built on the former laundry site.

St Luke's Hospital, off Warren Road, was built as the Guildford Infirmary within the town's union workhouse in 1896. It became Warren Road Hospital when Surrey County Council took over the infirmary and institution in the 1930s. This picture was taken in June 1992.

In this view a part of the boundary wall has survived and the postbox has been resited.

It was renamed St Luke's Hospital in 1945 – taking the title from the mission church that stood in nearby Addison Road. The hospital expanded and by the 1960s provided a wide range of health care services. Here we see the WRVS canteen and shop.

Today, a great deal of housing has been squeezed into St Luke's Park leaving few traces of how it all once looked.

As the new Royal Surrey County Hospital at Park Barn expanded, services, wards and departments were transferred away from St Luke's Hospital. The two hospitals became a combined NHS trust in 1991 and in 1997 phase three of the Royal Surrey opened as the St Luke's Cancer Centre, making the Warren Road site redundant.

Now the road that once ran through the hospital is a dead end. Away to the right, behind the trees and bushes, is the St Luke's GPs' surgery.

In 1919 Pewley Down was purchased by the Friary Brewery and given to the town on the understanding that it was to be kept as an open space and also in memory of those men from the town who had been killed in the First World War. A stone tablet was erected explaining this with a dial on the top pointing to surrounding places of interest and their distance in miles from this spot. One of those places was the Crystal Palace in south London, which, until it burned down in 1936, could be glimpsed from Pewley Down on sunny days.

A new stone tablet has been erected with a replacement dial. The views are as stunning today as they have ever been.

Children enjoy playing games in the sand at the top of St Catherine's Hill. In the middle foreground the River Wey meanders through the water meadows and beyond is the steeple of Shalford Church and the former Shalford House. The picture appears to date from the 1950s.

Shifting sands: It is surprising to see just how much sand has been eroded. The steeple of Shalford Church is still visible, but only just.

A puff of smoke and a blur of a train is caught through a gap in the trees by a photographer just after the First World War. It is indeed a pleasant composition with St Catherine's Chapel on the hill in the background.

The photographer of the accompanying picture found this spot by standing in a far corner of the grounds of Langton Priory off Portsmouth Road. Approached down a lane with its own bridge over the railway line, the building is now occupied by QDS, a company specialising in environmental consultancy within the property, petroleum and industrial sectors around the world.

A toll gate and keeper's cottage was erected on the Portsmouth Road in the 1760s. This photograph was probably taken shortly before the turnpike was discontinued in 1870. Guildown Road can be seen going off to the right beyond the gates.

And Guildown Road, beyond where the temporary fencing protecting the road works is, is the only feature that appears to have survived.

The Onslow Village housing scheme was started in 1920 to provide homes at a time of a national shortage. The Earl of Onslow sold the land at a quarter of its market value to the scheme and the borough council loaned the scheme £20,000. This view, looking down Wilderness Road, appeared on a picture postcard that was sent on April 26, 1923. Note the dairy cart with its milk churn parked in the road in the centre of the picture.

The copper beech hedges and other trees have been allowed to grow over the years, and this certainly complements the original vision which was to create a delightful garden suburb.

Westborough was originally known as the Aldershot Road Estate. The first homes were erected in the mid 1920s. By 1938, 372 houses and 140 flats had been built or were nearing completion. That year saw the opening of the 1,250th municipal house in the borough. Here, the houses in Fairfield Rise, off Southway, are nearing completion.

Fairfield Rise as seen today, but it is interesting to note that at the time when only half of Westborough had been developed, Bishop John Harold Greig (the first Bishop of Guildford, 1927-34), described it as one of the fairest housing developments he had seen.

At the crest of the hill along Southway looking in an easterly direction, before the road itself was laid. Although power tools and forms of mechanised transport are being used, earlier transport is evident. A horse and cart can be seen driving along the muddy trackway on the far right.

Without the older picture it is hard to image just how much landscaping was done here!

And looking in the opposite direction a temporary railway is seen with presumably a petrol-driven locomotive. It would have hauled the wagons that are being loaded with the heavy, sticky clay.

In recent years the scheme giving tenants the right to buy their council homes has resulted in many houses being extended and altered. Back in 1938 the borough proudly proclaimed that the convenience of each tenant had been fully considered. And owing to the attractive cost of electricity, electric cookers and wash-boilers had been provided, together with necessary heating points and aerials for wirelesses.

The end of the road in April 1945! The Westborough estate petered out at the western end of Southway and in the distance a lorry and some workmen can be seen.

Kings College, built as Park Barn Secondary School in the 1950s, along with much of the housing beyond, is the obvious difference between the two photos. And lines of parked cars and speed humps also characterise this busy road today.

Caxton Gardens, off Woodbridge Hill, soon after the houses were built in 1907 for employees of the Guildford printers Billings. For such a small housing scheme it was photographed and published on a number of different Edwardian picture postcards.

Little appears to have changed over the years (except the parked cars) and even the terracotta sundial remains. Billings was based in Walnut Tree Close and printed, among other titles, Bibles, in more than 200 different languages.

The bottom of Woodbridge Hill as it looked in the early 1900s with a steam train heading for London. A white sign post can be seen to the right and this almost certainly pointed the way to the isolation hospital that was beyond the Dennis motor works. This picture first appeared in the book *Images of Guildford* by David Rose and Graham Collyer that was published in 1998. The caption noted a photograph taken at the same spot in 1995.

And here it is, taken on a Sunday in March of that year when a steam-hauled special ran on the same line. The author had learned that the locomotive that day would be a former London & South Western Railway M7 tank engine, the same as the one in the previous photo. He couldn't believe his luck when it came into view, coal-bunker first, pulling its carriages enabling him to take a shot with an uncanny resemblance to the earlier one. However, the view has changed over the last 90-odd years – most noticeably the ugly concrete footbridge.

Worplesdon Road looking towards Woodbridge Hill in January 1979. On the left can be seen the offices of F. W. Francis, wine and spirit merchants. Before the Second World War, briar pipe and walking stick manufacturers Mason & Toogood had been based here. Cane for the sticks came from a copse beyond Pinks Hill near Wood Street Village. Victory Industries were here after the war.

Francis Court sheltered housing scheme has been added on the left and another house further down has gone to be replaced by a building called Parke House.

Nugent Hall was in Stoughton Road on the corner with North Road. Seen here in May 1981, it looks in a sorry state. The corrugated-iron hall had once stood in Worplesdon Road and was the forerunner of Stoughton's Emmanuel Church.

Here is another bit of infilling with a number of flats now occupying the site.

Drivers, conductors and other staff of the Yellow Bus Service pose with their vehicles outside the firm's Worplesdon Road depot on a wet day shortly after the end of the Second World War. In the background, on the corner of Barrack Road, can be seen the Royal Hotel and Sparrow's the butchers.

The last Yellow buses ran in 1958 and the garage building, seen here, has had a number of occupants since. These include Neilsons Ice Cream Depot in the 1960s, and in more recent times it has been a furniture warehouse. The BT phone box had recently been toppled when this photograph was taken.

A band of the Queen's Regiment marches out from Stoughton Barracks and down Barrack Road in a view that dates from about 1935.

With vehicles parked on either side of the road, it would be difficult to recreate the scene in the previous photograph today. The Army left the barracks more than 20 years ago and it has now been converted to housing with additional homes built within the grounds.

Youngsters enjoy a game of cricket inside the small park bordering Stoughton Road and New Cross Road, in about 1918.

Stoughton Methodist Church, built in 1895, is largely unaltered, and the main features that separate the two photographs are the shops on the corner of Grange Road and the fairly recent seating in the park itself.

The borough council developed the Bellfields estate after the Second World War, buying land that had once been part of the Stoke Hill Estate. A high wall had surrounded the estate – parts of it still survive to this day. This view, looking down Stoughton Road, was taken in January 1945.

The cottages whose gardens back on to the River Wey line up with those in the previous view to establish that the photographer of the accompanying photograph was standing near the entrance of the Jarvis clinic.

# SHALFORD

Shalford Road in the early 1900s and a view of the toll-keepers cottage. At one time tolls payable here were: "for every horse, mule or ass, laden or unladen", four pence halfpenny. And for "every score of oxen, cows, or meat cattle", the sum of seven pence halfpenny.

A Mr and Mrs Whitbourn were the last keepers of the toll house, but it had long been disused when it was pulled down during the 1930s at about the time the entrance to Pilgrims' Way and Shalford Road was widened. Today, front gardens and driveways face this side of the road.

Chantry Cottage from a picture postcard of about 100 years ago.

The cottage looks as pretty today as it did when the previous picture was taken. Some of the trees in the woodland behind came down in the Great Storm of 1987.

Chantry Cottage was once a gamekeeper's cottage on the Austin estate and looks to have been a rather remote spot about a century ago.

A line of fir trees currently obscure the cottage and the path seems to have changed direction. The houses along Pilgrims' Way are now close by and the small car park is popular with walkers.

A Guildford guide book from the 1920s advertised the Shalford Park Hotel and Golf Links, with park gardens and woodlands of 68 acres. Originally the home of the Austin family, it was used as a hotel from 1910 to 1938.

Before it was demolished in the 1970s it had been used as offices by Cornhill Insurance. Today Shalford Park contains a number of football pitches and is the venue for the Guildford Lions' Easter Show and as a concert venue. It has also been used for pageant plays.

Shalford's parish church, St Mary the Virgin, was just over 40 years old when this photograph was taken in about 1870. The house on the left is Debnershe, standing almost opposite the church on the Shalford Road.

Both views have been taken from a field near the junction of East Shalford Lane and Tilehurst Road. Very little has changed over the last 125 years.

Toco's Chintz Tea Shoppe once occupied the cottage facing the road. By the small green can be seen the sign and entrance to the Shalford Park Hotel.

The charming cottages remain the same but the tea rooms and the little sweet shop have long gone. The war memorial now stands on the green in front of the church.

The Seahorse became a pub in the late 18th century and had previously been a house called Burtons. For many years, from the 1930s onwards, it was under the ownership of the Horndean brewery George Gale & Co. In recent years its owners attempted to change the pub's name to the Wise Old Owl. There was much outcry and eventually the plan was sensibly dropped.

The view is mainly unchanged but may not have been had Hitler's troops invaded England during the Second World War. A road block, as part of the national GHQ stopline, was here and points such as this would certainly have seen much fighting if the enemy had reached here on its way to London.

High gables and tall chimneys were a feature of the station building at Shalford. On the left-hand side can be seen several cattle pens. The last regular steam trains on this, the Reading to Redhill line, ran in 1965. Since 1967, the station has not been staffed.

A railway station devoid of its main building looks somewhat odd. The footbridge and platforms are about all that remain.

"Motors & cycles" proclaims the sign above William Warns' shop and works. The canopied shop here in Kings Road was once Mills the grocers. A drinking fountain and horse-trough can be seen to the right of the telegraph pole.

Other traders may have come and gone, but Warns garage is still in the centre of the village. It was not until recent times that it stopped selling petrol from the garage forecourt.

Queens Hall in Station Road was built as a village hall by Guildford architect Henry Peak for Edward Ellis JP, in 1886. It was used to entertain soldiers during the First World War and during the Second World War was the HQ of the local Home Guard.

Today the Shalford village club still occupies the main part of the building, although some parts of it have other uses. The local Bryant family once had a grocers and tobacconist shop in the middle part of the building.

A view that goes back about 50 years with a rider and her two horses passing the post office in Kings Road. Note the two mothers pushing prams and the tin-plate advertising signs for Lyons cakes and Senior Service cigarettes.

Signs of the times today include one for photocopying, the large signboard above the Chinese takeaway and the current oval sign in use everywhere by the Post Office.

The Methodist Church in Kings Road is the focal point of this early 20th century picture postcard view.

The line of the buildings remain virtually unaltered and it is still a very pleasant scene viewed from across the village pond.

And looking in the other direction across the pond to Kings Road are a group of buildings named in the 1900s as Alexandra Cottages.

The telegraph pole has gone and one cottage in particular has undergone quite a change with a new style roof.

Looking across the common and in the distance can be seen the buildings along Kings Road. On the right is the Cricketers Inn – then a Lascelles, Tickner & Co Ltd, licensed house.

Still called the Cricketers, it is now a private house. The last pint of ale was served as long ago as 1936. In its latter years it was a Friary, Holroyd & Healy's Brewery pub.

Cows on the common with a man in a bowler hat and a boy with a pair of pails. No fences and on the road beyond no traffic either.

Nowadays the common is completely overgrown with trees and bushes, so the photograph has been taken nearer to the A281 Horsham Road, with Popular Road joining it in on the left of the picture.

# CHILWORTH, BLACKHEATH AND ALBURY

Chilworth has a long history of habitation – a mill at the time of Domesday Book, followed by gunpowder and paper mills along the Tillingbourne – but it was in the 20th century that houses began to line the main street through the village. Some of that development is seen here in New Road.

St Thomas's Church had previously been a working men's club for employees of the gunpowder works and Unwins paper mill. It was then conveyed to the vicar of Shalford and in June 1896 was licensed by the Bishop of Winchester as a place of worship.

The approach to Chilworth and Albury railway station seen here in the early part of the 20th century with plenty of paraphernalia to interest the railway historian by way of lamps, signals, iron footbridge, and so on! The station staff have turned out to have their photograph taken.

Nowadays the station is just called Chilworth and much of its original features have been stripped away – but not lost. The level crossing gates were bought by the Dart Valley Railway in Devon, while the footbridge was purchased by the East Somerset Railway, another heritage line that operates preserved steam locomotives.

Blackheath, with the village hall seen to the left in the picture, is without doubt a pretty spot surrounded by glorious heaths and woodland.

It is still a quiet village, with no major road running through it, but not as quiet as in the previous photograph taken more than 60 years ago.

Albury's old parish church stands in the grounds of Albury Park. It is by far the oldest building around with parts of the tower dating back to Saxon times. And also here was the original village. However, the church ceased to be used on a regular basis in 1842 when the new church of SS Peter and Paul was built and a new village grew up along Weston Street.

This delightful church fell into disrepair and for many years stood forlorn. Then, in the 1970s, its plight was taken up by the Redundant Churches Uses Committee and since then a sizeable amount of restoration work has been done. Services are occasionally held here.

The visitor to Albury can't fail to notice the elaborate chimneys evident on a number of its buildings. They are by the architect Augustus Pugin (1812-52), whose other great work is the Houses of Parliament.

Little appears to have changed from the accompanying circa 1920s view and today. However, what was once the village post office is now residential accommodation.

Another building with characteristic Pugin chimneys was the cottage that was also the village police headquarters. The man in the centre is Roger Parke who was an inspector with the Surrey Constabulary. The photograph is thought to date from the 1870s.

It is believed that the cottage was pulled down towards the end of the 19th century and replaced by the one seen here. It is near the sharp band of The Street and its junction with New Road.

The Drummond Arms dates back to 1830 and stands on the site occupied by an earlier pub that was known as the Running Horse. The Drummond family coat of arms can be seen above the first-floor windows in the centre of the building. Henry Drummond purchased Albury Park and its mansion in 1819. The name on the side of the wagon in this 1900s view is B. COE. The family had a farm in the village, while another branch became well known for growing watercress at Abinger Hammer.

Now painted white, it can also be seen that the Drummond Arms has undergone some structural alterations to the rooms on the upper floors. And today the coat of arms is featured on a metal sign.

Vintage views of pub gardens are quite rare, but this shows the one at the Drummond Arms in about the 1920s.

The garden leads down to the Tillingbourne stream and remains a delightful spot to relax and enjoy refreshments. Picnic benches have replaced the scattering of wooden tables and chairs in the accompanying picture.

The mill at Albury, seen here in the 1900s. There had been a mill on this site at Albury going back to the 13th century. However, its most infamous night came in December 1830 when it was set alight by a local labourer called James Warner. It was the time of the Swing Riots when there were many acts of vandalism throughout the countryside by workers who were in fear of losing their jobs by the introduction of new machinery. It is believed that Warner also fired shots at the miller's house. The unfortunate protester was caught and hanged for his crimes in January 1831. And some historians believe he may have been the last person in this country to be executed for arson.

The later mill was once owned by the firm Botting & Son. They eventually moved their business a mile or so further down the Tillingbourne to Lower Postford Mill. In recent years the mill buildings have been used as laboratories.

A fall of snow back in the 1900s brought out Albury-based photographer Percy Lloyd to take this picture of Birmingham Lane now called Blacksmith Lane – at the junction of Church Lane. Lloyd was a prolific publisher of picture postcards throughout this part of Surrey. He was also Albury's postmaster. The man in the picture is Bert Stedman, who carried Lloyd's equipment and drove his pony and trap on his photographic forays.

The lamp may have gone but the field gateway beside the old Round House cottage survives. The track leads to Albury Heath and then on to Blackheath, and all around is some of the most glorious countryside in the whole of Surrey.

Another local spot captured by the Albury-based photographer Percy Lloyd. Deep in the woods to the south of the village, it was reached by a path through The Warren, seen going off to the right in this early 1900s view. The woman standing by the gate is believed to be Mr Lloyd's wife, Elizabeth.

In Lloyd's day this place was known as The Paddlecombs. How often is it referred to by that name today I wonder?

The Silent Pool, a Surrey beauty spot known by many, took on a very different appearance in 1992 after a year of very low rainfall. Normally fed by chalk springs from the North Downs, it is a rare, but not a unique occurrence to see it devoid of water. Nevertheless it still drew visitors to the site, just off the A25 near the Shere by-pass.

There has been rather a lot of rain in the last couple of years and once again the Silent Pool looks its best. This was how the Victorian writer Martin Tupper would have known it when he featured it in his fictional story of a young girl's death by drowning in his novel *Stephan Langton or The Days of King John*. Unfortunately, the story has passed into local folklore and for generations the sorry tale has been re-told as if it were the truth.

The cottage beside the track to the Silent Pool was a once a tea room. It did a roaring trade as visitors flocked to the beauty spot here and at nearby Newlands Corner.

The author can remember back to the 1960s when it still sold refreshments, but it is now a private house. However, the paths and wooden walkways around the Silent Pool itself are in excellent condition and nearby Sherebourne Farm, with its collection of animals, is open to the public for family visits.

The road south from Albury goes over the heath and drops down towards the small community at Brook. Here there is a level crossing on the Guildford to Redhill railway line. When this photograph was taken, prior to the First World War, the crossing was manned by a keeper whose wooden cabin can be seen in the picture.

Automatic barriers replaced the old hand-operated gates many years ago, and the house seen on the right in the accompanying photograph has gone – destroyed in a fire. Will the heath soon become an area of woodland?

# WONERSH

The name Wonersh is thought to derive from the Anglo-Saxon words 'wogen' meaning crooked or winding, and 'ersc' – a stubble field. This early 1900s view of the then sleepy village looks down The Street towards Bramley.

Interesting to note that today the half-timbering and whitewashed rendering on the buildings is far more pronounced than it was in the early 1900s.

By the 1500s the village had a thriving cottage industry producing woollen goods known as kersey. The boom years did not last, however, and like the rest of the West Surrey wool trade, it fell into decline following years of accusations that the cloth was being deliberately stretched when dry. Thus the unsuspecting buyer would get a surprise when it shrank back to its original size when wetted! This view, also from the 1900s, looks in the opposite direction to the previous pair of pictures, towards the centre of the village.

For the photographer seeking an enchanting view in the centre of a Surrey village, it is unfortunate that here, as in other villages such as Shere and Abinger Hammer, that it's almost impossible due to the lines of parked cars. On the other hand, very good for an historian faithfully recording the scene in 2003!

These four pictures show the changes to the village centre and the Grantley Arms pub. Here, in about 1900, a pair of horse-drawn delivery vans appear to have paused for a while in the middle of the muddy road junction. A couple of youngsters seem to be the only ones interested in what's going on.

The Pepperpot is the best known feature in the village. It was given to the village in 1929 by Robert Haslam, who at that time owned Wonersh Park. It is thought that the beams came from the mansion itself and the tiles from an ice house that stood in the grounds. The house, formerly the home of Lord Grantley, was pulled down in 1935. Today it is an open space called Church Green.

The Pepperpot looked a very sorry sight after it had been hit by a lorry back in April 1983. It was not beyond repair and was painstakingly restored. However, as Wonersh resident and local historian Ron Hill notes, it has been damaged by passing vehicles no less than six times in the past 25 years. The last one being in 1991. It has had its width reduced and now stands on a solid plinth. The Pepperpot was intended to be used as a bus stop – but not today though, due to the speed of traffic passing through the village! There have been plans to relocate it, but these were met by howls of protest from villagers.

The Grantley Arms is a lovely old half-timbered building that may date back as far as the mid 17th century. It is named after Fletcher Norman, First Baron Grantley (1716-1789). Born at Grantley in Yorkshire, he was both a colourful and dubious lawyer and an MP. His wife was Grace, the daughter and heir to Sir William Chapple of Green Place, Wonersh. Lord Grantley did rather well for himself both financially and professionally, securing a number of top government positions including that of Speaker of the House of Commons. There has been a number of changes to the pub over the last 100 years, as seen here, notably the left-hand side portion of the building.

A row of cottages on the road to Wonersh from Shalford. The diamond shapes on the wall of the end cottage formed by dark blue header bricks is known as a diaper pattern.

The view has not changed a great deal although the ditch has been filled in.

# BRAMLEY

Bramley Grange was originally called The White House and was built for a Mrs Parsons in 1878. A Captain Webster purchased it in 1886 and redeveloped it as a mock-tudor residence renaming it The Grange. With its 230 acres of land he ran it as a 'gentleman's' estate. In 1920, Lt Col Miller, on demob from the army, acquired the building and converted it to The Bramley Grange Hotel. From 1924 to 1969 it was owned by the Elfbank Syndicate and over the years there were numerous extensions and alterations. It was in private ownership until it was taken over by Alexandra Hotels in 1986.

In 1992, The Bramley Grange went into receivership. Its major creditor, the Bank of Scotland, purchased it and it continued to trade under the operating name of Englefield Hotels. Its fate changed yet again when on the night of March 3, 1996, it was destroyed by fire. Today, what remained of the hotel has been cleared away and retirement apartments are being built on the

St Catherine's School for girls opened with 11 boarders and six day pupils on September 25, 1885. A major fire caused much damage on April 11, 1904, when a bolt of lightning struck a metal flagpole. Luckily, it was during the Easter holidays and no one was injured. However, a large crowd soon gathered to watch as firefighters tried to smother the flames. A number of photographs were taken and published soon after as picture postcards.

Over the years the school has expanded considerably and is still an independent day and boarding school. It now has more than 500 pupils. Its 100th anniversary was celebrated with the completion of the Centenary Building that houses the sixth-form and a lecture theatre. The up-to-date photograph was taken on Good Friday, April 18, 2003.

A delightful Edwardian view with the inn signs clearly visible of the two pubs in the village – the Jolly Farmer and the Wheatsheaf. Many years ago the former had also been called the Wheatsheaf, when, the latter was a pair of cottages. They were converted to a beerhouse during the 1880s.

Apart from one or two cosmetic changes to the buildings, the view is largely the same.

Another Edwardian picture postcard view and here we look along the High Street with a terrace of shops on the right-hand side. Langrish – The Bramley Stores is advertising Gilbey's Wines and Spirits. It later became the Forest Stores and then a branch of Fine Fare.

An antiques shop now occupies the building described in the previous photo; and although a satellite dish, indicative of modern times, can be seen further down the row, also evident is a barber's traditional striped pole.

This view is from the opposite direction and would appear to be a little later in date that the previous photo. It captures a platoon of soldiers with a number of horse-drawn limbers. Note Jackson's Cycle Works on the right. This was run by Ted Jackson, whose brothers were also in the cycle or motor-vehicle trade. The name is certainly well known locally. Ernest Jackson had a cycle shop and motor-garage in Guildford, Bert owned a garage at Hurtmore, Charlie had a garage at Compton, and George ran a garage in Horsham.

The side of the road where Jackson's Cycle Works once stood has seen several changes with new buildings added here and there although the opposite side remains much the same.

This three-storey building facing the High Street at the eastern side of the village was the Bramley Brewery, owned by William Smith. Beer was brewed here from 1865 to 1904, when it was bought by Bruford's Cranleigh Brewery, along with its eight licensed houses. William's brother Richard also owned an iron foundry on the same site.

All the buildings have survived but their usage today is very different – a showroom selling exclusive cars being one of the businesses now operating from here.

Moving further along the High Street in an easterly direction and we reach some of Bramley's fine villas standing behind walls and hedges. The motor-car would suggest that this is a picture from the 1920s or 30s. The building on the right had been the original shop of the once well-known Bramley electrical firm of Robertsons.

The addition of some white posts on the right appear to be the only difference between the two pictures.

The railway from Guildford to Horsham was opened in 1865 and lasted 100 years. The main station building at Bramley, seen here, included the station master's house. He could be the bearded man standing fourth from the left.

Today the building is gone except for the letter box that now stands alone at the entrance to the Bramley Business Park that opened in 1992.

In earlier times the line was mostly operated by "push-pull" trains. The train could either be pulled in the normal way by the locomotive at the front, or the driver could sit in a compartment at the end of the second carriage and allow the train to be propelled in the opposite direction by working air-pressure controls. Time-consuming shunting movements were therefore unnecessary at the end of each journey. This train is about to leave for Horsham.

The scene can be traced today as one of the platforms is still in place. Now the trackbed is part of the Downs Link public footpath, popular with both walkers and cyclists. The car park is a useful rendezvous for those exploring the path.

The official title of the station was Bramley & Wonersh. Dating from the early 1900s, this is a lovely photograph of the station staff in their London & South Western Railway uniforms. But who is the man on the far right? He may have been from "head office" at Waterloo and was visiting on the day the photograph was taken.

The unprofitable line closed in 1965 as part of the cuts to Britain's railways by Dr Richard Beeching. It was, however, one of the few to do so in this part of the country. In recent years there have been plans put forward to re-open it from Guildford as far as Cranleigh. The likelihood at this moment does not look promising. However, there are a number of reminders of the old railway on this site – including this station sign.

A view along a leafy Station Road on what appears to be a glorious summer's day in Edwardian times.

The green and white enamel station sign has been returned to Bramley courtesy of the parish council. It was bought from a dealer in Sussex who obtained it from a resident of Kemp Town, Brighton, who had been using it as shelving in his greenhouse. Fortunately, it has survived in excellent condition. It's interesting to note that life at a branch line station was far removed from those on the main line. For instance, further down the line at Baynards, the signalman grew 1,000 dahlia plants in flower beds along the platforms. And if you needed a haircut, you could drop into the signal box at Bramley & Wonersh where the signalman carried out an unofficial second job!

# SHERE

Shere is without doubt one of the most picturesque villages in Surrey. But as these views will show there have been several changes to the delightful buildings around the village square over the years.

The "old view" dates to between the two world wars. This is still one of the classic "chocolate box" views of Surrey, but almost impossible to photograph without it being obscured by vehicles.

The junctions of Upper Street, Middle Street and Gomshall Lane and a close inspection of some of the rendering on the cottages on the left shows that at this date prior to the Second World War it was in need of some attention.

The original brickwork is now the preferred option for the cottages on the left. Note that on the half-timbered building that is currently an antiques shop chimney pots have been added to the stack.

An Edwardian view down Middle Street with the bridge over the Tillingbourne Stream in the foreground. Could the man on the bridge attending to the horse standing in the water be the village blacksmith?

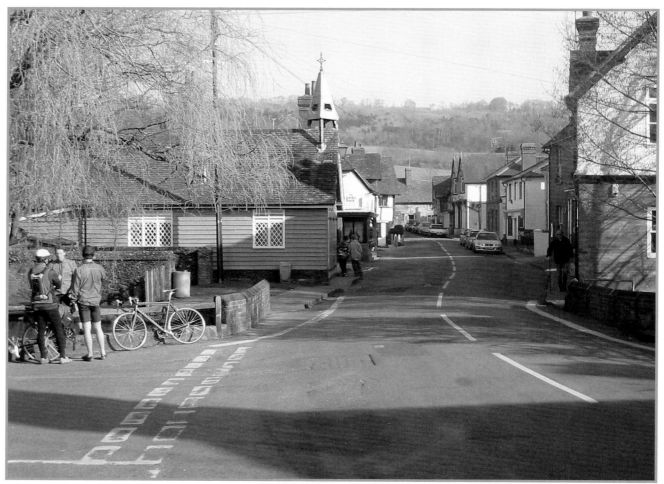

The same view early on a Sunday morning in 2003 before the village has filled up with visitors. Nevertheless, the sunny weather has brought out a group of cyclists who have stopped for a rest.

The White Horse, one of the village's two pubs, was originally a farmhouse built in about 1500. It became an inn during the 17th century and once had its own brewhouse. The two horses have their nosebags on and it is likely that the cart is delivering mineral waters and ginger beer. The year is about 1900.

The current timberwork may look old, but would appear to be a 20th century addition. Several years ago, a TV drama series set during the Second World War featured the White Horse pub. The outside of the building had something of a make-over and there were several scenes of American servicemen in the village square. However, scenes that were supposedly set inside the pub were filmed at a studio miles away and, of course, bore no resemblance to the real bar of this enchanting hostelry.

Back in the 14th century, Christine the Anchoress was locked up inside a tiny cell in Shere church for three long years at her own request and by permission from the Bishop of Winchester. This unusual choice was due to her extreme belief in Godly obedience and chastity. A small aperture through which food and drink was passed was her only contact with the outside world.

St James' Church is as quiet and tranquil today as it probably was then. The older photograph was taken in the 1900s. The church has a rich history indeed and dates to the 12th century at least, but may be even older.

A view from the church looking back towards the centre of the village.

And 50 years on from the accompanying photo, little has changed in this corner of Shere.

# GOMSHALL, ABINGER HAMMER AND HOLMBURY ST MARY

The tanning of leather was an important trade in Gomshall from the 16th century up until 1988. Tannery buildings stood behind those seen here in the 1900s. The tanning industry's heyday was during the 19th century when the business was owned by the Evershed family.

The plain flat-fronted building is now painted pink, fawn and cream, and stands out rather well. It makes an interesting comparison with the photograph of yesteryear.

This is a most charming picture postcard view taken by Albury photographer Percy Lloyd. Dating from the early 1900s, one wonders how long it took him to position all the children in what appears to be the perfect spot before he pulled the hood of his tripod-mounted camera over his head and released the shutter.

Has time eroded a charming view? Or is it because we are looking at a bygone era through "rose-tinted" spectacles? Note: there were buildings of a commercial and industrial nature on the left-hand side 100 years ago.

Most mills in these parts were built several stories high. However, Gomshall Mill is unusually long and low. Its construction is due to its twin water wheels both having horizontal drive shafts instead of the normal vertical ones. The mill was still grinding corn in 1951 when J. Hillier wrote his classic book, *Old Surrey Water-mills*.

Following refurbishment, the mill became an antiques shop and then a warren of gift and craft shops. In recent years it has become a restaurant that is part of the Blubeckers chain. Inside, some of the original wheel mechanism has been preserved and you can still see the waters of the Tillingbourne rushing under the building.

The Black Horse is another familiar building in the centre of Gomshall. Reffell's Brewery was once here and part of it can be seen behind the main building. The inn was purchased by Young & Co of Wandsworth in 1926, who demolished the brewery building three years later.

For some years it had been Mulligans fish restaurant, but today it is a public house again with a restaurant serving Thai cuisine.

Abinger Hammer with its unusual clock is a well known spot. In this picture, from about 1900, the building that was once a blacksmith's shop is seen with a previous timepiece attached to its wall.

The current clock, featuring the figure of a blacksmith who strikes a bell each hour with his hammer, dates from 1909 and was given in memory of the first Lord Farrier of Abinger Hall. However, the hammer in the name of the village is a reminder of the ancient iron industry that once occupied these parts.

High up in the Surrey Hills is Holmbury St Mary, a scattered settlement among some glorious pine woods. Once a very remote part of Surrey, much of the development can be traced to the Victorian period after the railway had reached Dorking, a few miles away.

For dedicated cyclists, the lanes through the hills around here are excellent. Compared to the previous picture, the conifers inside the churchyard have grown rather tall and nearly obscure the lynch gate.

As the community grew, so St Mary's Church was built in 1879. To the right is the Royal Oak pub which once sold Reigate Ales brewed by Mellersh & Neale.

The sign board above the pub has gone but the village has a sign post, erected in 1992 to mark the 40th anniversary of the Queen's ascension to the throne.

One of Holmbury's older buildings is the Kings Head pub, that may date back to the 17th century. Local public house historian Mark Sturley says that it once had its own brewhouse. In this 1900s view some likely customers appear to be making their way up the road.

A part of the village that would appear to be just as quiet as it was 100 years ago. The necessity to create a car park probably saw the removal of the wall and note the porch is quite different from the one in the previous picture.

# MERROW

Sub-post offices seem to be disappearing faster than ever these days, and here is the one at Down Road, Merrow, that went several years ago. This picture dates from about 1980 and note the chocolate machine on the front wall. Similar vending machines, including those for cigarettes and chewing gum, once very common, have also all but gone from local shops.

The shop carried on for several years as a sub-post office and gift shop known as Out of Town. Currently, the premises is used by solicitors and members of the public can drop in for legal advice.

The village hall was built in 1909 and is seen here a decade or so later.

Surprisingly there have been few alterations to the outside of the building. Today, it also contains a social club with a bowling green behind; while the hall is used for all manner of functions and is regularly hired out for what are advertised as "psychic fairs".

Epsom Road looking east at about the time of the First World War. An up-ended cart can be seen in the middle distance outside the village forge.

All the buildings in the accompanying picture appear to have gone and the scene is almost unrecognisable. The location has been pinpointed using old maps and noting that the site of today's fuel station was once the site of the forge.

The Bushy Hill estate was built in Merrow in the 1950s and the shops in the centre of this 1977 picture had been added by the mid-1960s. On the right can be seen the premises of A. C. Stiles, ironmonger and hardware dealer, who traded in the village for many years.

The hardware shop has become an Indian restaurant among a number of different traders here now. However, the main difference has been the widening of the road, the addition of bollards and the repositioning of the bus shelter.

The church and pub at Merrow have afforded a good composition for photographers for many years. Seen here in about 1900, the Horse and Groom was once known as the Running Horse – a name no doubt associated with the annual Whitsun week Guildford Races held from 1701 to 1870 on Merrow Downs.

Also a well-known landmark scene on the approach to Guildford, St John's Church has features dating back to the 12th century, although it underwent much rebuilding in 1842. In 2002, after a successful fundraising campaign, the war memorial in the churchyard was refurbished. To celebrate the event there was an extremely well attended rededication ceremony.

The little girl sitting in the cart is being pulled by a donkey to the top of Merrow Downs and Newlands Corner from the direction of Shere and Albury. The man holds the reins and there is no one else in sight on the road, or on the grassy slopes, in a picture taken about 100 years ago.

Today it is the busy A25, but still affords some glorious views. A difficult location to pinpoint accurately as there have been many changes in the growth and then the cutting down of trees and bushes. However, the road appears to follow the same course.

# Clandon and Horsley

The great house at Clandon Park was built by the Venetian architect Gracomo Leoni in 1731 and the grounds were laid out by "Capability" Brown. It has been the home of the Onslow family, of which three members have had the distinction of holding the position of Speaker of the House of Commons. During the First World War, at about the time this photograph was taken, it became a hospital for injured servicemen.

Today Clandon Park is a National Trust property. Open to the public and showing off its fine rooms it is also home to the Queen's Regiment Museum. These views look in a westerly direction (beyond today's car park) and show the rear of the house.

West Clandon's church is dedicated to Saints Peter and Paul. Although standing beside the road that runs through the village, it is actually in Clandon Park itself. Inside the church there are a number of memorials to the Onslow family who have been here since the 17th century.

Part of the flint wall around the churchyard seems to have disappeared, and there is now a wind vane on top of the church spire.

The Street at West Clandon from a picture postcard sent from the village to an address in Devon in 1904. The third building from the left is the Bulls Head pub, a building that may date back as far as the middle of the 16th century.

The Bulls Head has not succumbed to a modern name change and the street looks much the same.

The "New Line" from Guildford to Waterloo via Cobham opened in 1885 with Clandon as one of its stations. Trains were operated by the London & South Western Railway and in this 1900s view the roadway approaching the station appears rather muddy. As can be seen on the left, old train rails had been used as a makeshift kerb.

Amazingly the station buildings have hardly changed and the only modern additions to the scene are the electric street lamps.

The 20th century writer and naturalist Eric Parker described Horsley Towers as "a little exotic among these stretches of Southern English parkland," adding "good Jacobean red-brick much better suits oaks and beeches than the chateau-like towers of a Scottish castle". The towers were the creation of the Earl of Lovelace along with other features in and around East Horsley in the middle of the 19th century. For reasons unknown, the signwriting on the side of the vehicle has been masked out on the original of this 1920s photograph.

The large tree in the foreground has been allowed to mature and today the building is used as an upmarket conference centre, complete with hotel and leisure facilities.

Members of the Surrey Union Hunt gather outside the Duke of Wellington pub at East Horsley on February 3, 1910. As they pose for the photographer a number of locals look on.

Although the pub may date back to the 1820s, the style in which it appears today – brick and flint – has much to do with Lord Lovelace's mid-19th century alterations. Internal modifications have taken place in recent times.

East Horsley, looking towards Station Approach, on a picture postcard that on the reverse side is postmarked 1943. The shop on the left is the wine merchants Tyler & Company – originally a Woking-based firm that by the 1960s had 163 shops in and around Surrey.

The same shop is currently an off licence and today, what was once The Horsley Hotel, further down, is now a restaurant. The slip road with parking bays reflects the age where the majority of locals drive to their nearest shops.

No one has done more by way of research and writing about the history of the Horsleys than Pam Bowley. She has had 12 books published full of local facts. She notes that in the years following 1380 there was much rebuilding in West Horsley. The Old Cottage on The Street is one such house that remains to this day and was one of the first to be built after the Black Death.

A wall now surrounds the property and trees partly obscure the neighbouring houses.

Looking south along Shere Road just past its junction with the main A246 Epsom Road. A few cottages have been built in this view that probably dates to the years before the Second World War.

This road takes the traveller on towards the North Downs and the beautiful woodlands at Sheepleas.

# RIPLEY AND SEND

In his book *Highways and Byways* of Surrey, Eric Parker noted: "Ripley itself, but for the traffic, would be the prettiest village on the road." This was 1908! And he added: "Ripley may look its best on a Saturday morning, before the flood rushes down the road. When the little village is clean and fresh in the sun, and its inns are busy with their white table cloths and cooking potatoes, and the children sit on the edge of the green. Before the dust comes, there is a sense of orderly bustle and of waiting for a day of hard work and good money that is pleasant enough."

Only a madman would spend more than a few seconds standing in the middle of this busy road today! But the view does afford a great deal of charm, including the parish church of St Mary, greeting visitors entering from the direction of Guildford. The new houses on the right are built on the site of the former village school.

In the latter part of the 19th century Ripley was a mecca for weekend cyclists from London – and The Anchor was the inn that most of them headed for. Here they were welcomed by its owners the Dibble family. Over the years thousands stopped there, signed the guest book, and enjoyed an excellent supper and refreshments. This picture is from the motor-age and teas are being advertised for the visitor to the village.

This interesting old building has retained much of its character and is still a popular watering hole. The Dibble's association with the Anchor ended in 1930. However, they are still remembered by a window dedicated to them in Ripley Church.

The inn sign of the Ship can be seen on the left-hand side of this picture postcard that is postmarked August 23, 1948. Always a haunt of locals rather than the travelling public, landlord John Pullen, who was there from from 1870 to 1895, made his own tables out of solid elm so that they couldn't be lifted and hurled through the windows by rowdy drinkers!

Today the street scene is crowded with motor vehicles, while the maturing trees also "fill in" the view.

At the other end of the village is the Talbot Hotel – its history going back centuries when it may have catered for visitors to nearby Newark Priory. It was a popular coaching inn on the London to Portsmouth road following the passing of the Turnpike Act in 1749. It is also rumoured that its once famous guests included Samuel Pepys, and also Lord Nelson and Lady Hamilton. This photograph dates to about the pre-Second World War years.

The brick facade, still seen today, dates from the 18th century, but the majority of the building is earlier, from the 16th century, with some parts believed to be even older. It has succumbed to a couple of fires in latter years. One, in the late 1980s, was the day before the author was supposed to be appearing there as the singer of Sammy Rat's Big Big Blues Band. There was much smoke damage in the bar, yet a poster on the wall advertising the band showed not the slightest effect of the blaze. Spooky!

St Mary's Church, Send, stands near the water meadows of the River Wey some distance from the main thoroughfare of today's village. Close to the church is the tomb of Dr Richard Stoughton, who made his fortune by his Great Cordial Elixir of the Stomach. He trained as an apothecary but was not a qualified medical practitioner at all, although he called himself a doctor. However, his quack remedy was selling so well by 1712 that he took out a patent to prevent others copying it. Whether his wonderstuff really did as it claimed – "to fortify the stomach after a bout of heavy drinking, clean the blood and expel wind" we will never know, but it did give his descendants a headache after his death in 1716; as for years afterwards there were legal rows over the true formula of the elixir and who had the rights to the patent.

The churchyard today is as tranquil a spot as any in this part of Surrey.

The Wey Navigation from Weybridge to Guildford is 19 and a half miles in length and was opened in 1653. It was the brainchild of Sir Richard Weston of Sutton Place, but unfortunately he did not see his waterway completed. It utilises sections of the natural river and "cuts" dug through the landscape at points where the river meanders or becomes too shallow to navigate. Near here are Walsham Gates, a flood lock, where the real river is joined by a section of canal from the direction of Weybridge.

Still a completely rural and tranquil spot that can be reached by following a footpath from the green at Ripley.

Triggs Lock, west of Send and near to Sutton Green, is another quiet spot on the Wey Navigation. The small lock-keeper's cottage dates from 1769 and one of its 19th century keepers raised a family of nine children here.

The scene has not changed much over the 50-odd years that separate these two views and the cottage still has no access to a public road. It is owned by the National Trust who, since 1964, has been responsible for looking after the entire waterway from Weybridge to Godalming.

Writing at the end of the 1950s, J. Hiller, said of Newark Mill, near Send: "I know of no other building so completely at one with its surroundings. Seen at the height of summer, it seems typical of the landscape and consorts perfectly with the slow river, the broad fields and the lazy cattle." At the time he was also worried as he observed that it was falling into decay. He warned that unless care was taken "there may come a time when restoration will be too late".

Unfortunately, there was little time left to do anything about the building, as on the night of December 3, 1966, Surrey lost one of its most impressive landmarks when the mill caught fire and was burned to the ground. And although the view looks attractive enough today, many who pass this way probably do not realise what a wonderful building once stood here.

# THE RHS GARDEN AT WISLEY

Wisley is a place known to gardeners everywhere. Covering some 240 acres, the Royal Horticultural Society's Garden at Wisley is one of the world's great gardens, with some of the largest plant collections to be found anywhere. The pergola on the right was removed in the mid 1980s and this picture was taken a few years earlier.

The garden was a gift to the RHS in 1903 by a wealthy Quaker, Sir Thomas Hanbury. Sixty acres of it had previously been owned and gardened by businessman, scientist and inventor, George Fergusson Wilson, a former treasurer of the RHS. In his day it was called Oakwood. The perfectly manicured lawns are a Wisley trade mark of the high standard of horticulture visitors have come to expect.

Here we look towards a north-facing slope a few years before the Rock Garden was created on it in 1911. It took three years to complete and a light railway was laid from what is now the A3 to transport the large blocks of Sussex sandstone. Its creator was landscape gardener Edward White.

The Long Pond at the foot of the Rock Garden appears much the same today. It is fed by a number of natural springs that emanate from the crevices between the rocks. Major renovations were carried out in the 1980s when parts of the Rock Garden were restored to their original design.

It may come as a surprise to many visitors to learn that the Laboratory building is not so old as it may look. It was, in fact, built between 1914-16, using reconstituted materials from old manor houses. It was designed by a London architectural firm with the unusual name of Pine-Coffin, Imrie & Angell.

Consisting of narrow brick and oak half timbering, the Laboratory houses botanic and scientific staff, and includes offices and a lecture theatre. Note the newer path on the left that is absent in the previous view that dates to about the 1950s.

Some features would appear to have been there as long as the garden itself. Not so with the Canal. From 1905 until 1969 rows of glasshouses were situated in front of the Laboratory.

The formal canal was designed by Sir Geoffrey Jellico and Lanning Roper. Full of fish, it also contains a wonderful collection of waterlilies.

The potting shed is now The Loggia situated at the end of the Canal. Seen here in about the 1950s or early 1960s, the shed was certainly a hive of activity.

It is now a walkway between the Canal and the Walled Gardens. Today, RHS Garden Wisley employs more than 270 people. A total of 83 are garden staff, the remainder working in the scientific, educational, administration and retail departments. In addition, each year there are 33 student gardeners and many volunteers.

An early 20th century view that shows the Long Pond in the foreground while looking towards a dense planting that also includes shrubs and trees created most likely by the earlier gardener George Fergusson Wilson.

This area is now the garden's Alpine Meadow – at its best in spring and early summer when it is covered with thousands of naturalised plants. But Wisley is a garden for all seasons as testified by the thousands of visitors who flock there each year to enjoy its beauty or simply to gain inspiration for their own gardens, large or small. Many are members of the RHS, which allows them to tap into its vast horticultural advisory and educational services.

# WORPLESDON

St Mary's Church with its fine tower has stood at this commanding position at the top of Perry Hill for centuries. Like many others it succumbed to a number of alterations in Victorian times when a Norman font was disposed of.

To stand in exactly the same spot as the original photographer would have resulted in a view of the church obscured by trees. This view was taken a few paces to the right.

The lane leading from Merrist Wood up to the main Guildford to Bagshot road. The earlier White Lyon pub can be seen in the distance with the tower of the church behind.

Merrist Wood House was built in 1881 and after the Second World War became an agricultural college. The college now offers a wide range of courses for land-based industries. This particular lane is no longer a through road.

The parish of Worplesdon is large and fairly spread out with communities including Wood Street Village, Jacobs Well and Fairlands. Perry Hill is the name of this part of the parish that runs alongside the A322.

These buildings at the top of the hill, opposite the Worplesdon Place Hotel, appear to have changed very little over the last 60 to 70 years.

Although Fox Corner is usually referred to as being in Worplesdon, it is in fact just inside the parish of Pirbright. A quiet enough scene here, but during the First World War – at about the time this photograph was taken – the area would have been busy with soldiers, many in tented camps on the nearby commons.

In the previous photograph the pub was owned by Simmonds Brewery of Reading. In 1960 it became a Courage house. The small outbuilding, once a gentleman's lavatory, still stands (out of view beyond the hedge).

The delightful green at Wood Street Village, in the parish of Worplesdon, in about 1930 when there was a small pond at the Frog Grove Lane end.

It is believed that Wood Street is the only Surrey village with a traditional maypole. Local children dance there each year on the nearest Saturday to the 1st of May, and also at the annual village show in July.

Looking in the opposite direction across the green at Wood Street towards White Hart Lane on the far left. The building with the pitched roof was once a wheelwright and blacksmith's shop.

From 1937 to 1954 the former wheelwright's shop was the home of the Wood Street branch of the Royal British Legion. During the evening of June 2, 1953, the day of the Queen's coronation, it was, according to the *Surrey Advertiser*, "lit by hundreds of coloured lights, providing a fairylike setting for the local celebrations". Now it is a private house.

# PIRBRIGHT

Pirbright with its large green away to the right, circa 1910. The road going off to the left leads to St Michael's Church, where lies the Welsh-born American journalist Henry Morton Stanley. It was he, who in 1871, finally tracked down the Scottish explorer Dr David Livingstone on the shores of Lake Tanganyika in Africa. In his later life Stanley lived at a house just outside the village.

The road has obviously been widened and the trees and fences have gone, but the view across the green has hardly changed.

Geese on the green about 100 years ago. There is still a pond on the green and still geese – now Canadian geese along with other wildfowl. Henley Park residents Lord and Lady Pirbright paid for the building of Lord Pirbright's Hall, seen here to the right. The hall was presented to the village on May 27, 1901, to mark the accession to the throne of Edward VII. In 1897 they donated a delightful drinking fountain to mark the diamond jubilee of Queen Victoria. It still stands beside the hall facing the road.

Some alterations have been made to the hall over the years as can be seen by comparing the two photographs.

Trees lined the green in days gone by. In the distance can be seen the White Hart pub a lovely old building that dates back to the 17th century.

There was plenty of controversy surrounding the pub a few years ago when its owners decided to change its name to the Moorhen. Villagers and the parish council fought in vain to keep the old name, but have now erected a sign on the green opposite that reads "White Hart Corner". However, the name change was nothing new as in fact, the building had once been called Lane End House.

# NORMANDY, ASH AND TONGHAM

The direction of the shadows would suggest that this photo, looking along the Guildford Road in the 1900s, was taken in the early afternoon on a fine day. On the right is the village store that sold all manner of items and was at one time a post office.

Moving on nearly 100 years and it just so happened that the present photograph was also taken on a particularly warm and sunny day, April 11, 2003. Since 1959 the shop has been home to a motorcycle business.

There appears to be some activity at Wanborough railway station in this 1900s view with a train from Guildford waiting and another arriving in the distance. Although the line opened in 1846, Normandy did not get its station until 1891. Prime Minister William Gladstone's private secretary, Sir Algernon West, was living at nearby Wanborough Manor and the house became a meeting place for politicians. It was therefore decided that it would be useful to have a railway station nearby.

The concrete footbridge was added in 1938, and since the late 1980s the station has not been staffed. Now the station building has been let for business purposes and the coal yard too has disappeared.

Once a thinly populated agricultural community, Ash grew rapidly after the army camp was established just across the county border at Aldershot in Hampshire in 1853. Seen here are Lickfold's Cottages and the village forge, providing a long-gone glimpse of an earlier, quieter age.

Nothing appears to link the old and the new except the Forge Works – a motor-vehicle repair business that is off the main road. The on-coming white car has just past the signs to it.

The railway came to Ash in 1849. Its station and engine shed were built by the South Eastern Railway that ran trains through here from Reigate to Reading via Guildford. This view is from 1986 when there were concerns that the shed had been earmarked for demolition.

At the time it was one of only two engine sheds in that style still standing, the other being at Lynmouth in Devon. However, it was not long before the Ash shed's owner, Roger Kendall, allayed any fears, saying that it would be kept in as near as its original condition as possible, and would be used for motor vehicle repairs. And so it is to this day.

The Victoria Hall in Ash Hill Road was built in 1897 to commemorate the diamond jubilee of Queen Victoria. It is seen here in about 1930.

The hall's foundation stone had been laid by Dr Henry Chester, who had bought the land for the hall to stand on. In 1998, while building work was going on, the foundation stone was removed and a time capsule found. Inside a large glass pickle jar were 1897 copies of the *Aldershot News* and *Sheldrake's News* and a selection of coins of the same year.

St Paul's Church in Poyle Road, Tongham, was consecrated in 1866. It may take its name for the simple reason that seen across the fields is the church of St Peter at Ash. These two saints being closely connected and recognised as important leaders of the early Christian church.

With about 40 years between the two photographs some small changes can be discerned. This view also takes in the unusual free-standing bell tower erected in 1899. It originally contained 13 tubular bells that rung a carillon that was said to sound like sheep bells. In 1957 these were replaced by a set of electronically-operated bells.

Looking west along Poyle Road a short distance on from the church with the Village Institute seen on the right. Once a coffee house and then a welfare centre, it was last used as a meeting hall in 1972. On the left can be seen the gateway to the vicarage.

The original 19th-century vicarage stood some way back from the road, but its coach house and stables have survived and can be seen on the left just behind the trees. Housing has replaced the institute.

# PUTTENHAM

Nestling at the foot of the south slope of the North Downs is Puttenham, a delightful village with a hop-growing tradition that continues to this day. This is an undated photograph but the old-style road sign warning motorists of a school must date it to more than 40 or 50 years ago.

The very same view looking east along the village street towards the church. Some of the walls, fences and hedges have changed and so too has the road sign!

Bicycles can be seen propped up against the wall of the Good Intent pub. Perhaps they belong to some local workers who have dropped in for a pint. The picture dates to about the 1930s.

A largely unchanged view in what is still a delightful Surrey village. The tile hanging on the extreme right must be a more recent addition.

The Puttenham junction along the Hog's Back in the days before the road was converted to dual carriageway. Earlier times of motoring are evident with an old-style AA box and even a patrolman standing by the side of the road waiting to salute members of the organisation as they drive past.

Alterations to the carriageway in both directions have made it difficult to pin point the exact spot as chosen by the previous photographer. And with traffic continually roaring past, you would not want to stand here for long these days!

# COMPTON AND LITTLETON

The church of St Nicholas at Compton is one of the most interesting you could wish to find. It has a unique double sanctuary on two levels, one of the earliest pieces of church woodwork to be found in this country and an equally early fragment of stained glass. However, its wonders do not stop there. Look for the picture of a Norman knight carved into the chancel arch near the pulpit, and on the outside south wall a small hole with scratch marks radiating from it. A metal gnomon or a wooden peg would have been inserted in the hole and the time of Mass and other services could have been told by the shadows cast across it by the sun.

Some of the trees beyond the church have gone so that the view now reveals part of Eastbury Manor, that is now a nursing home.

Watts memorial Chapel, completed in 1904, was funded by the artist George Frederick Watts and designed by his wife Mary, in the Italian Romanesque-style. They lived nearby at Limnerslease. Mary Watts encouraged and taught villagers to create the Celtic terracotta symbols that adorn the chapel and to paint the intricate panels on the inside walls.

Grade I listed, the chapel was in need of urgent restoration by the 1990s. Funds were raised locally and £21,000 of lottery funding from English Heritage have helped restore this beautiful and unusual building. Currently, trees in the churchyard unfortunately obscure it when standing at the same spot from which the accompanying picture was taken.

Evening classes where local people came to learn arts and crafts techniques proved popular and these led to the formation of the Compton Potters' Arts Guild. During the first half of the 20th century terracotta garden ornaments, plus a wealth of other wares and ceramics were produced on a commercial basis at the pottery here. Judging by this 1920s view, it appears to have had a number of visitors who came by motor-car. Some of the pottery buildings can just be seen through the trees.

G. F. Watts died in 1904 and was buried in a tomb near the memorial chapel. His wife died in 1938 and is buried alongside him. The pottery continued until 1956. However, the gallery is open to this day and houses a fine collection of both Watts' paintings and sculptures and work created by the potters at Compton.

Standing out rather majestically here in about 1900 is White Hart Cottage. It has been dated to 1520 and tradition suggests it was once a church ale house. Allegedly, it gained the name White Hart Inn after the night a fowler, creeping across the meadow opposite, caught sight of a beautiful snow-white hart.

Little change here. However, Cecilia Lady Boston, writing in the *History of Compton in Surrey* (1933), noted that the property had "in recent times, occasionally been referred to as Chittys, from the fact that an old Mr Chitty worked on the ground level there as a cobbler".

A smithy had been on this site in Compton for centuries. One of the large elm trees, seen here in about 1900, had developed an unusually wide girth. For many years horses standing next to it waiting to be shod had chewed its young shoots and that had resulted in the tree continually trying to grow more shoots near its base.

Set back from the road, a shop selling antiques is here now, and also a cottage named The Forge.

The Harrow appears to have become a licensed house in the 19th century, but the history of the buildings on this site goes back as far as 1607.

The pub may not have changed its outward appearance but the wall and bank on the opposite side of the road has gone and has been replaced by a sloping grass verge.

The hamlet of Littleton is closely connected with Loseley Park whose land is all around it, but a number of its buildings are older than Loseley House itself. This 1920s picture shows the timber framed cottage Long Meadow. The origins of the house go back to medieval times and it was once the home of a yeoman farmer. In later times it became a pair of cottages, but is now a single property once again.

Owing to the fact that the hedgerow has grown so much, today's picture was taken just inside the field. The small church of St Francis can also be seen. Services are held on special occasions and the 19th century building was once a school house. The barn, seen to the right, is newer, but nevertheless is an old building. It had originally stood in Wiltshire but was dismantled and re-erected here in 1982.

Littleton Lane, looking south, in the early 1960s. Some of Loseley's famous Jersey cows are leaving the milking parlour at Orange Court Farm.

The most noticeable changes appear to be the trees on the left-hand side. Although cows are no longer milked here some of the farm buildings are used by local shepherdess Chloe Dancey for her rare breeds of sheep.

# EASHING

Eashing Bridge is one of six similar structures that span the River Wey upstream from Guildford. It is thought that they were built by the monks of Waverley Abbey after previous bridges were destroyed by a great flood in 1233. Tilford has two bridges, the others are at Elstead, Peper Harow, and Unstead.

Traffic lights control the single-line of traffic that is permitted to cross the bridge today.

This view was taken from the bridge itself in the early 1900s. The National Trust bought it along with the cottages on the left for £400 in 1902. There was a mill here at the time of Domesday Book in 1086 and it was probably the building named in the survey as Pipereherge. Much altered over the years, the structure that stood on the site in the 20th century suffered a serious blaze in 1916 and again in 1932.

A sizeable development of commercial properties has just been built on the old mill site. The units are now ready for occupation.

Here we look along the stretch of road that leads from Eashing towards the A3. There was once a blacksmith's shop on the left, but here the driver of the car would certainly have been enjoying the days of motoring when, in this part of Surrey, the open road really was just that!

Another change that has come about as roads have become busier is the ubiquitous white lines in the middle of our "country lanes".

The Guildford to Godalming bypass was built during the 1930s and provided much-needed work at a time of great unemployment. It attracted workers from many parts of the UK. This is the thatched-roof petrol station at Eashing beside the then new A3.

Those who break their journey to visit this service station while travelling along the A3 today may like to consider the thoughts of Eric Parker, who wrote about the same stretch of road soon after the Second World War. "Of all the bypasses which I have come to know in Surrey, I like best the road that runs from the Milford crossroads, avoiding Godalming, to Guildford. All the way you are in the countryside. More, for you see different sides of Surrey – sand and chalk, willow and elm, water and distant hills. And of the months in which to see the bypass happiest in the sun I should choose June."